Family Matters

David L. Smith

Linda H. Smith

ROYSTON
Publishing

BK Royston Publishing
P. O. Box 4321
Jeffersonville, IN 47131
502-802-5385
http://www.bkroystonpublishing.com
bkroystonpublishing@gmail.com

© Copyright – 2020

All Rights Reserved. No part of this book may be reproduced, stored in a retrieval system, or transmitted by any means without the written permission of the author.

Cover Design: Elite Covers

ISBN-13: 978-1-951941-59-8

Scripture from the King James Version. Public Domain

Printed in the United States of America

Dedication

We dedicate this book to our children: Tamara, Crystal and Jessica as they have been a family support throughout our tenure in ministry.

Acknowledgements

We acknowledge our Lord and Savior Jesus Christ who has been the center and source of our Family.

We also wish to acknowledge our grandparents and parents who showed us what family looks like.

Table of Contents

Dedication	iii
Acknowledgements	v
Introduction	vii
Chapter 1 God's View of the Family	1
Chapter 2 The Roles of the Family	11
Chapter 3 Alternative Families	23
Chapter 4 Separation, Divorce and Remarriage	33
Chapter 5 Grandparents Raising Grandchildren	45

Chapter 6 Aging, Alone and Abandoned Families	57
Chapter 7 The Family in Crisis	71
About the Author Pastor David L. Smith	87
About the Author First Lady Linda H. Smith	91

Introduction

In today's society, family is defined in so many ways. There is the family that is related to you by blood and birth. There is the family that you adopt in place of that family that you lost due to death or disagreement. There is the family that adopts someone else's child when they are unable or unwilling to care for the child. A new family that may not look like you or have your same DNA but over time, the love that connects binds closer than natural blood. There is the family that is developed over time in a company with a unit of employees who have just bonded while working for the profitability and success of a business but becomes a family. There are also the scary family ties that come with being members of gangs, violence and other detrimental groups that seek to harm others to gain power and position. This may not be your family that you are a member of but they do exist. It's sad but true that there are people willing to die instead betray these groupings that have formed to resemble and duplicate a 'family.' Recently, we have seen in the news the heart wrenching results of families literally torn apart at the border. Political view points and opinions have taken over and the humane ability to protect and not divide a family of an innocent child even though they are an immigrant is no longer sacred. Children taken from the arms of their parents because they were willing to risk everything to come to a country in hopes of a better life. What will these children's family look like in the future? How will they recover emotionally, physically and spiritually from these seemingly in humane acts of political mandates? We can't solve all of the problems in the world, only God can. Our job as a church and ministry is to somehow lead them to God, be the hands and feet of God to help, support and love the families that God places in our path.

We pray that this book would help you in your everyday journeys of life. Our experiences have taught us that there are no shortcuts as it relates to building relationships in the family.

Satan knows every trick in the book as he goes to and fro trying to destroy the family;

however, God has ordained the family. If we obey the Word of God then there is no problem too hard for God.

As you read this book, our hope is that you trust in the Lord with all your heart lean not to your own understanding but in all your ways acknowledge Him and He shall direct your path. Proverbs 3:5-6

When you believe the Bible is entirely true, then you allow it to be the foundation of everything you say and do. A Family that Prays together stays together!

Pastor David L. Smith

First Lady Linda H. Smith

Chapter 1
God's View of the Family

The website www.dictionary.com defines *family as a basic social unit consisting of parents and their children, considered as a group, whether dwelling together or not.* This definition is specially labeled, traditional family.

The second definition is *a social unit consisting of one or more adults together with the children they care for.* This definition is specially labeled, single parent family. For us to get a clear view of what God says about the family, we have to go to His Word in Genesis. Why? In the beginning, God created Heaven and earth. (Genesis

1:1)*[1]He created everything that exists so we must return to the Creator to find out about His creation. What did the Creator have in mind when he created man, woman and the family? What was the purpose of the position that He placed mankind in so that he hopefully would be able to prosper?

Throughout the chapter of Genesis 1, we see how God created everything including the water, darkness, light, fowls that flew in the air and every living creature that moves in the sea. God created all of the vegetation, land and water masses. He decided where the water would stop and the land would begin. God created it all. In Genesis 1:27, the Bible tells us that God

---

*[1] All scripture quotes are from the King James Version of the Bible unless otherwise noted.

created mankind in His image and likeness. He created male and female to reproduce after their own kind. Therefore, there was a male animal and female animal created by God to be fruitful, multiply and reproduce in the earth.

In Genesis 2, God rested from all of His labor in creation and said it was "good." God also created Eden. Eden was a perfect paradise. Throughout Chapter 2 of Genesis, the Word talks about how wonderful Eden was with all of its trees, produce and mighty rivers. Eden was where man was to dwell, inhabit, multiply, commune with God and have dominion over every living creature. God created Adam out of the dust of the ground, put him in Eden, and gave him an assignment to name all of the animals. God had to have given Adam the brain power and knowledge to know what to call each animal. He had provision, intelligence and dominion, but not one of the animals was a companion for him. Adam had no partner, helpmeet or lover to unite with and reproduce like the animals. Finally, God put Adam to sleep and took a rib out of him and formed a woman. Adam said when he looked at Eve that this is bone of my bone and flesh of my flesh. Genesis 2:23, Adam and Eve became one flesh both were naked and unashamed. (Genesis 2:24–25)God created them both and presented Eve to Adam. God created them and then united them. His plan was man for the woman and woman for the man, together as one. In the words of the marriage ceremony, "I now pronounce you husband and wife." This is the first family. Everything was wonderful in Eden. All that Adam and Eve needed was provided for them in Eden. There was food, water and an assignment from God to have dominion over this perfect place. Adam had someone to love who loved him in return, and, finally, God's constant communication, guidance and love. Life was perfect. But there was one thing they could not do and that was to eat of the tree of the knowledge of good and evil. The only restriction He placed in Eden was not to eat of that single tree. They had access to everything else but that one tree. There were specific consequences for Adam's actions if he disobeyed God's command. "He would surely die." (Genesis 2:16–17) Adam could not eat of that one tree. No problem at all right? Wrong. In Chapter 3 of Genesis, the introduction of the serpent and his plan that was against God's plan changed everything. Not to mention that the serpent approached Eve, the woman, instead of Adam. Adam received the commandment. Eve did not. Eve was deceived by the serpent and gave the fruit that she ate to Adam. Once Adam ate the fruit, the perfect life in Eden was over. The troubles of the family began with that one act of disobedience to God. Sin entered the perfect world that God had made. Man was immediately dismissed from the perfect place in Eden. Man would now experience death. Man would have to work for everything. Woman would now have the work and pain of childbirth as well as to be a helpmeet for the man. This was not the original plan of God. The original plan was for man to have dominion, not work. In Eden, there was plenty and not any lack. Because of their perfectly created bodies by God, there should not have been any pain, just purpose. Now the first family must face eminent death, challenges of survival, take on new roles and assume positions in the world that they have no choice but to accept because of their actions and God's law. This was not God's divine plan. Just think, God gave the commandment to Adam first and since Eve did eat and offered the fruit to Adam to eat, Adam should have resisted the temptation, went to God, and asked God to forgive his wife for her disobedience. Maybe the outcome could have been different for the first family.

Reflection Page

Reflection Page

Chapter 2
The Roles of the Family

In sports, every player on the field or in the arena has a position to play. Whether you understand the rules of the game; the plays in the game or the well-known players of the game, the objective is to win. No matter if the sport is hockey, soccer, field hockey, water polo or the more known sports of football, basketball or the All-American sport of baseball, every player has an area to cover, responsibility, strengths and weaknesses. In sports, it's about playing a game, either professionally, collegiate or for leisure. With regards to our families, this is not a game, this is life. Each person's position or role, as we will call it for our discussion, in the family is important and critical to the survival, success and thriving of the entire family structure. Everything hinges on the family. The success of our homes, schools, churches, communities and world will rise and fall based on the family. As we stated in the earlier chapter, we will always refer to the Bible for the model and standard for our families. I realize that our modern families may not reflect the initial intent of the family that God had in mind. Nevertheless, God's Word is still our standard, guide and example of what He intended in the world even until today. The first question we will address here is the roles of each family member. Now before we begin, we realize that some of the roles that some family members should assume are not assumed for various reasons. Our time together in this book is not to degrade any role or person that may have been missing for whatever the reason. Our purpose is to point out what God originally design each person's role to be. In today's families, how a person assumes those particular roles may look altogether different.

The Man's Role

The man was given his role by God Himself. Why? In the beginning God formed man from the dust of the ground. **Genesis 2:7** He told him to have dominion over the garden to take care of it. Adam was to name all of the animals and be in relationship with God. **Genesis 1:26** God then realized that Adam was alone because there was no beast suitable for him so God put Adam to sleep and took a rib out of Adam and made the woman. **Genesis 2:22** After the woman was introduced to Adam, God said, "Be fruitful and multiply." **Genesis 1:28** So, the order of God for the first family was for the man, Adam, to be the head of the household. Not only was Adam to be the provider for the household but the spiritual leader for the entire household. Remember the fall of man didn't happen until Adam partook of the fruit that Eve gave to him. The original covenant was between God and Adam. Adam was created and designed to be the leader and head of his household. Since Adam was created in the image of God, he and Eve were perfectly made. They were also in the garden unashamed; there was no need to hide anything from God because he created them both and they were naked. **Genesis 2:25**

When God created them both, He said it was Good; they were Holy, pure and righteous. **Genesis 1:31** Since God ordered them to be fruitful and multiply, He also created sex which is in perfect order as long as it is within the confines of the family and marital structure that God Himself created. Thus, this is God's order for the family. We may not see this structure much today with the man as the head of the household but it is still God's way.

The Woman's Role

We have established that the man's role is the head of the house. The woman's role is to be a helpmeet for the man, conceive and bear children, as well as be the lead when keeping the home. Now one of the most controversial terms in the human language for the biblical family relationship is in the New Testament, and it refers to submission. "Wives, submit yourselves unto your own husbands, as unto the Lord." (Ephesians 5:22) Most of the time the women in the church or congregation cringe at this scripture. But the scripture in James 4:7 states "Submit yourselves therefore to God. Resist the devil, and he will flee from you." This scripture refers to both the man and the woman. So, the woman is not the only one that has any submitting to do. The man also should submit himself unto God. But for structure in the family and order in the home, we all submit ourselves unto God.

The wife should submit herself to her own husband and then the children will submit to their parents. Submission is about order and structure not about abuse, misuse or domination for control. For when a Godly man is submitting himself unto God, hopefully, wanting the best for his family, loving his wife as God loves the church, there should be less concern about the wife's willingness to submit to her husband. Now a very smart man will pray to God, realize the capacity and strength of his wife, and work together as a team similar to any great sports team to get the win for their household. Submit means to place or rank under authority. No matter the wife's strength, ability, finances or position, she should never disrespect her husband because his position biblically is still the head of the household. She will give him his proper respect as the spiritual leader by praying with him for God's direction and guidance. Additionally, the Godly husband will fully respect his wife and understand that her role as the wife is not to be positioned under his feet but standing right beside him for strength, comfort and support. One more scripture on submission before we move on, "Submitting yourselves one to another in the fear of God." (Ephesians 5:21) God is serious about how we treat each other however within the structure of God's family, He is the head of us all. If we all submit to Him, everything else will have order and fall in line according to His plan and will.

The Child's Role

The child's role is to be a child. The parents' responsibility is to train up children in the way they should go, nurture children with love and care, as well as discipline, structure and direct them in the way that they should go. (Proverbs 22:6) First the children should be directed to love and fear God. Secondly, children should be disciplined in the ways of God and the household. Finally, through love and disciple from God children will display their training as they move forward. Thus, children should surrender under the authority of their parents. (Ephesians 6:1) The mother is submitted under the authority of the father. The father should submit unto God and the house should be in order according to God's will and plan. Anything that is not in that order, will be out of order. Things that are out of order within the home will create chaos, confusion and ultimately division within the family.

This question must be asked, "Is your home out of order?" What are the steps that you will take to get your home back in order?

Reflection Page

Reflection Page

Chapter 3
Alternative Families

If the original version of something is perfect, why do you need anything else or even think about creating an alternative? In the Garden of Eden, man and woman were created in God's image and likeness. God himself said that it was good. But with the fall of man from Eve's deception by the serpent, sin has entered into the world, now God's plan, people and path have been altered. God didn't change, but His creation has changed forever through disobedience and sin. Over the course of time, man, woman and the entire family structure doesn't look or function the same. There are survival skills, hardships, combined with man's own imagination and desires that have created families God did not initially intend to exist. Now we are faced with a reality in this society of a family dynamic that doesn't look like the original plan of God. Daily as a church and body of Christ, we must address these family dynamics, minister to them and love them as God has commanded.

Throughout the Bible and no different than today, we see that children/young people are being raised by different family members under many different circumstances. Moses was raised in a palace. He wasn't born into royalty, but God's plan and the path He had his birth mother take, gained him access to the princess of Egypt. She fell in love with him in a basket in the river and thus he become a prince of Egypt to save Israel, God's chosen people from Pharaoh, slavery and bondage. Moses became the Prince by adoption and not by birth but definitely, by necessity.

Esther, who became queen in a foreign land, was raised by her uncle Mordecai. The Bible doesn't tell us exactly what happened to her parents, but Mordecai guided her throughout the process of her rise to be queen. In the New Testament, Paul was the mentor to the young preacher and pastor Timothy. Paul often talked about Timothy's influence, guidance and upbringing by his mother Lois and grandmother Eunice. Timothy's father was not mentioned in Paul's discourses. Where was the father? There are millions of young people today who ask this same question about their fathers. I, myself, was primarily reared by my mother and grandmother. My father was not in the picture but I was highly influenced by deacons in the church, coaches in sports and other strong male role models. It is not the same as your own father but it is an alternative. It was probably not my mother or father's original intent as well as our heavenly Father, but there are circumstances beyond our control that force us to do our best in unpredictable situation. Human beings are very resourceful, especially women, who seek to give their children, especially their sons the best that they can. In today's society, many of our minority fathers and mothers are incarcerated and unable to see their children on a regular basis besides monthly visits. Other fathers choose to not be connected to their children because of their children's mother. Eventually some fathers begin all over creating other families with new women, leaving a hole in the hearts of children asking themselves, "What's wrong with me?" Unfortunately, there are a number of fathers who are deceased, which makes death, not jail bars, a divide between children and their fathers. Gun violence, drug involvement and, sometimes drunk driving accidents have created fatherless families. What do we as the church do now? How do we carry the gospel to a generation(s) that are missing one of the key elements of the gospel; the Love of the

Father? Some people have a hard time with the gospel because they didn't have the correct example or any love from a father or father figure. Having a father is a foreign idea and some people don't make the connection well. The roles we talked about in the last chapter have never been seen by some of the young generation. Does this negate the Heavenly Father's role, care or love for His children? Not at all. Does His love diminish or stop being poured out just because it is not received? Not at all. Our job as a church and ministry is made much more difficult and we must be sensitive to the fact that some terms such as father, mother, child and their respective roles are not seen or understood.

Now to take the alternative family one step further, there are now grandparents taking care of and raising their grandchildren.

It is no longer just the single mothers but now single grandmothers/grandfathers are responsible for their grandchildren. Not to mention the guardians willing to cross cultures and ethnicities, foster care, other extended family, adoptive families and the church, community and villages everywhere willing to help to raise and nurture children around the world. Where would some of these children be if they didn't have these alternative families? War, disease and poverty are other factors. In the end, we are all a part of an alternative family. The family of God. The Israelites were God's original and chosen people but thankfully, through Jesus Christ, the Cross and Grace, we have been grafted into the Family of God. Thanks be unto God. What is the church's response? Love. We are to teach God's original plan for the family and what each of our roles should be in the family. God is still the head of us all. The father should still be the head, spiritual leader and covering for his family. The mother is the helpmeet to the man, spiritual support, leader and caretaker of the children inside the home, as well as subject to her own husband. The children are still to be subject to their parents. This was God's original intent. But if for some reason, your family doesn't look like this, the church should still love, greet, uphold, teach and train you God's Way. God is still Holy and the Bible is still God's Word. Heaven is still for everyone that believes. Hell belongs to the devil and his angels. The church is still a hospital for everyone to receive the Savior, His healing, hope and family love.

# Reflection Page

Chapter 4
Separation, Divorce and Remarriage

"It hath been said, Whosoever shall put away his wife, let him give her a writing of divorcement." Matthew 5:31 (KJV)

Divorce is not new. We see the "Bill of Divorcement" mentioned in the scriptures. So, there is truly nothing new under the sun.

Today, according to the website [www.gillespieshields.com,](www.gillespieshields.com) in 2020, that 60% of couples married between the age of 20 and 25 will end in divorce in the United States. Although statistics for divorce are high for ages 20-25, the church is always hopeful and prayerful that divorce will not occur. But in a lot of cases, it is when they will divorce because 60% is more than half. It is sad for the children and all who are connected and possibly will become disconnected in that relationship as a result of the divorce. So, the church has to be ready. As much as the church schedules pre-marital counseling sessions, singles events, engaged couple events and retreats which take place in churches around the world, prior to and after the weddings, it is realistic that separation and ultimately divorce is a strong possibility. Why might you ask? Because people change, don't change, or put in the work that it takes to make the marriage work. At times, the couple may have been advised not to get married at all but they ignored the advice and married anyway. What happens next? They come back to the church with a bigger problem than where they started. Why is it a bigger problem? Because the woman may have had a child by this man; there were children involved prior to the marriage; there are financial ties such as property, pensions, retirement and 401K plans; relationships in the church and extended family — which makes everything messy and confusing. Ultimately, there is hurt, misunderstandings, arguments, division and then divorce.

What should the church do? Keep teaching, training and counseling to the best of their ability and budget. If there is not a trained person in the church, go and partner with a community leader, counseling professional or other private groups that will work with churches to provide that help and assistance. In a lot of cases, they could be a guest speaker for an honorarium who will also offer their professional services by accepting certain insurance benefits.

In other cases, the church has to seek to not take sides, especially if the man and the woman or their extended family is a part of the church and active in the church fellowship. This is difficult because even though the church wasn't responsible for the couple's breakup, the church can be held to blame if one of the parties is active in the church especially in a highly visible role. If infidelity has occurred in the relationship, should the leader take a less visible role for a short time and then return to his or her normal leadership role? Some more traditional churches have done an actual "'sit down or silence" of leaders, and they have been asked to come before the church in the case of infidelity. This is all very difficult on all parties including the pastors, leaders, family, wife, husband and children. In a smaller to medium size congregation, this can be extremely difficult and cause a congregation to go through a divisive, grieving and unloving atmosphere. The worship can possibly be affected as well by the lack or decrease in the Holy Spirit's ease of movement throughout a service, which is desperately needed for healing, deliverance, restoration and the overall direction of the pastoral leader and the church. The Holy Spirit can move regardless of any circumstance, but where there is disunity, division, unforgiveness, bitterness, strife and anger, we can grieve the Holy Spirit by not having the pure heart that He needs in which to work more freely and easily.

What happens if the husband and/or wife after the divorce, gets remarried? Now there is another set of circumstances that must be considered because now there is a remarriage and now another person has entered the situation. The children may be torn between the father, mother, the stepmother or stepfather. If they are all in the same church, that can be even messier because of the potential for disagreement or all of the parties become uncooperative. So, what is the church's role in these circumstances? Love everyone. That is the new commandment that Jesus gave for all of us which is to love everyone, our neighbor as ourselves, Love your enemy and Love those who despitefully use you. Love is powerful but it requires maturity and strength. Love is an emotion but the love in a storm or struggle is not an emotional feeling but it's related to an act of faith and the Holy Spirit. Your natural man doesn't want to love someone who hurt them but Jesus told us otherwise, that we have to Love. "He that loveth not, knoweth not God; for God is Love." I John 4:8 (KJV)

Now as much as we preach and teach to work at staying together as a family and avoiding separation and divorce, if two people cannot get along and there is fighting, bickering or any level of abuse, we do not condone that a person stay and subject themselves and their children to abuse of any kind. We don't believe that God intends for any person to be abused verbally, physically, spiritually or emotionally by their spouse. We don't believe that it is God's plan for anyone. Seek help. Get to safety, protection and seek medical attention. On the other hand, the abuser needs counseling and help as well for their problem. After the professional help, it does not mean that the individual must return to the spouse after seeking the professional services unless he/she can be assured that he/she is safe and the person has indeed changed. Abusive behavior is not God's way. God is the head of the church, the man is the head of the house and the wife is the helpmeet but the Bible says in Ephesians 5:25 (KJV) "Husbands, love your wives, even as Christ also loved the church, and gave himself for it;" Then in verse 28, "So ought men to love their wives as their own bodies…." So, if the husband loves his wife as he loves his own body, he should not be abusing her because normally he should not be abusing himself. In the last phrase of verse 28 of Ephesian 5, "He that loveth his wife loveth himself." That's an answer right there for someone not loving or seemingly having the capability of someone else because they don't love themselves.

Divorce and separation are a sign of loss, brokenness and ill-repair that will result in a period of grief by all parties for what once was and may never be again. As the church, we have to continue to teach, give examples of potentially wrong relationships and realize that being unequally yoked has multi-facets and detrimental consequences.

Reflection Page

Reflection Page

Chapter 5
Grandparents Raising Grandchildren

In a recent Grand Facts Reports (which is a Fact Sheet study along with data from the 2010 census in a collaborative effort of the American Association of Retired Persons(AARP), the Brookdale Foundation Group, Children's Defense Fund, CWLA, Generations United and the Casey Family programs) stated that almost 7.8 million children under the age of 18 are living in homes where the householders are grandparents.

https://www.aarp.org/content/dam/aarp/relationships/friends-family/grandfacts/grandfacts-national.pdf

Additionally, that same Grand Fact Sheet stated that more than 2.5 million grandparents are responsible for their grandchildren living with them. The cultural or ethnic breakdown of the grandparents is 51.1% are white, 24.2% are African American/Black, 18.7% are Hispanic/Latino and 2.9% are Asian or of Asian descent. That's a lot of grandparents taking care of, providing for and housing their grandchildren. For more information on the statistics listed on a state-by-state basis, that information is located at http://www.grandfamilies.org/State-Fact-Sheets.

We have traditionally thought that the children and grandchildren would take care of the long-term care and funeral arrangements of the grandparents, but currently, that is not the case. The grandparents are now having to start all over again raising the next generation and possibly their children, which is two generations after them. There has been a saying that, "I love it when the grandchildren come over because I can send them back home." But today, in a lot of cases, the grandchildren are not coming over from their house: the grandparents' house IS their house.

First, we must say that we commend and congratulate those grandparents raising grandchildren. In some cases, the choice is either for the grandchildren to live with the grandparents or go into foster care. That is a real situation that a lot of young children/youth find themselves in. Both parents are unable, unwilling, deceased or absent for the care of their own children. Why? Multiple reasons. The age of some of the parents when they gave birth to their children was way too young or they were immature and unable to handle or provide all of the necessary financial, emotional and stabilizing needs for their child. In the past twenty to thirty years, the drug trafficking and gang culture led to a high incarceration rate especially in the African American and Latino communities, thus the father and possibly the mother is not there to care for the child or children. Educational and limited work qualifications have required that some of these parents still be living in their parents home with their child just to make ends meet. It's a complicated situation on all sides of the scenario. The grandparents have lost their freedom, their privacy of an "empty nest" is gone, the added expense of water, gas, heat, internet access, food, etc., with more people in the house and possible conflict in the raising and discipline of the child. The parents of the children, on the other hand, are possibly embarrassed or uncomfortable with the idea that they now have to go back home to their parents' house that they lived in as a child, but this time not alone but accompanied by their own child. Ultimately, the children have no say. They are children with no job, resources or legal options to take care of themselves and must go along with whatever, whenever and whoever is in control of the situation. It leads to so many feelings, emotions, behaviors that may or may not be common to the personalities of any of the people involved but now everyone's life is turned upside down and it causes a multitude of things to occur. Domestic violence, homelessness, anger, strife, bitterness, hopelessness and in some cases, suicide.

What is the church to do?

First, we must love and pray for all parties concerned. "That men ought always to pray and not to faint," (Luke 18:1b) or "Pray without ceasing" (1 Thessalonians 5:17) are two immediate scriptures that come to mind. Second, we have to love all parties concerned: the grandparents, parents and the children. After that, it's time to act. Creating a culture, systems and outlets of support for this group of people in the church. In Chapter 7, we will talk about families in crisis and the impact of the recent global pandemic because even though we may not be able to physically gather in large groups, we must continue to connect, collaborate and keep in contact with our church family and extended family to give them what they need.

What do we all need now?

Spiritual support and connection are especially necessary during difficult times in life that we all find ourselves in. No matter how the service is aired or shared, make sure that people are able to hear, feel and see the gospel of Jesus Christ continuing to go forth. Hearing the Word builds faith in God which in turn gives us all the power, strength, courage and wisdom to move forward with daily living. "So then Faith cometh by hearing and hearing by the word of God." (Romans 10:17)

Create ministries and sub-groups that address the needs of the grandparents, specifically. They need people to talk to who understand today's children and what their habits, needs, desires and outlets are. What worked twenty to thirty years ago may not work today. The actions, activities and access that children today want is totally different from what children did yesterday. Now, we know that "Jesus Christ the same yesterday, today and forever," (Hebrews 13:8) but human beings and especially the young people of today are not the same. How they feel, what they want, what they think they need and what they will do is totally different from what our generation would think, do and want.

Partnering with other families that have young children as a support group in addition to the church wide activities and support. There are single people with no children at all who don't have a clue or understand the struggle and needs of not only people with children but grandparents with children. Grandparents are not as vibrant, active or attentive as younger parents are or should be and thus it is a struggle and taxing on the body, mind and spirit to take care of very active young people.

Now it will be easier and more engaging when the in-person activities can return to normal along with the after school activities, sports, Boys and Girls Club programming, summer programs and other community activities will resume. Until then, the cry for support is heard and must continue to be heard for these grandparents because in the end, it will decrease the mental and physical health of the grandparents who are responsible, and thus the grandchildren will be more at risk than before. This will force them to become wards of the state, passed from one family member's home to the next and susceptible to all types of temptations that the world has to offer. But, with God, the church and the community's help and support, we will help our grandparents as much as possible to see the next generation survive and thrive to be the children of God and community citizens that they were meant to be.

Reflection Page

Chapter 6
Aging, Alone and Abandoned Families

The Bible clearly tells us and promises us long life to those who serve God. "With long life will I satisfy him and shew him my salvation."(Psalm 91:16) The Bible also states that in Proverbs 20:29: "The glory of young men is their strength: and the beauty of old men is the grey head." In another Proverb, "Gray hair is a crown of glory; it is gained in a righteous life." (Proverbs 16:31 ESV)

To age is a gift from God and a promise for the righteous, but to age and not be well taken care of, "seen after" as the generations before us said or to be loved and communicated with is not a gift but a shame.

Paul instructed Timothy to "Honor widows who are truly widows."(I Timothy 5:3 ESV) So it is the church's responsibility to honor, check in on and keep them protected and assisted with the resources that the widows or widowers, especially without children or grandchildren, need to live a comfortable life in their older years. Those widows with children and/or grandchildren who can care for them are not to be overlooked in anyway, but the care for them is different because they do have family to see after them and meet their needs. The Bible is very clear on the widows and the elderly to receive a certain level of respect and honor. Historically the Jewish community is very respectful of their aging men and women and throughout scripture, it admonishes us and teaches us that the older women are to teach the young women how to love their husbands and take care of their children so those who are older among us are not to be ignored, shunned or discarded in any way.

There are other aging people who need special care and are not able to stay in their own home or with their children or grandchildren. They are admitted into a nursing home facility or assisted living facility to receive the care, safety and protection that the elderly need. This group may still have visits from their family members and although they may live alone, they are not necessarily lonely. There are many people who live alone in these facilities or in their homes because of their choice and not necessary totally alone. Even in the assisted living and/or nursing home facilities, there is a responsibility to check on each resident on a regular basis. Not to mention that the other residents make a consorted effort to check on each other whether it is asked, wanted or not. Community living is just that, a community living under one roof and the interaction and engagement with each other is constant. Again, although these people live alone in their own apartment or condo, they can live very social and active lives.

On the other hand, there are people who are actually alone with limited communication and socialization with other entities and people besides the church. There are people whose families have actually rejected them and will not communicate with them for one reason or another. There are others who are alone because their biological family is unknown due to adoption and catastrophic death and demise. There are some people who choose to not communicate or have interaction with their family members because it is for their own safety and security. It is possible to be found in all of these categories: Aging, Alone and Abandoned.

In Chapter 5, we talked extensively about the grandparents raising grandchildren and showed statistically how low of a percentage the Asian grandparents were raising their grandchildren. Why?

Because in the Asian cultures they have traditionally revered their older generation of adults or grandparents. Very rarely will you go into a nursing home and see someone of Asian culture or descent. They are not there. There is a family member assigned, appointed and who has accepted the responsibility of taking care of that family member until they die. This culture has traditionally honored their parents and the elderly that way.

This is not an accusation of any one or another culture or group of people. There are many who are taking care of their aging parents, family members and extended family with dignity and quality care. As a whole and as a culture, Americans have not kept that honored habit, tradition and adjustment to their own lifestyle to take in a family member and care for them. Why? We work and the family may still be left alone because of long work hours and other responsibilities. The economy is such that both parents, older children and anybody else taking up space and occupying the home must work. So, the family member who is very ill and even lives with family, will either have to have in-home care or to be left alone at times. Is that the best place for them? Probably not especially for those with dementia. Alzheimer's patients are sometimes the most at risk and can easily walk away from the house and be lost or disoriented. Some have even died because they left the house not properly dressed in very bad weather, etc. So, what can the church do to help these people and families who find themselves with loved ones who need extra care in their aging years or may find themselves temporarily or permanently alone and abandoned?

First, we should love them, pray for them and if necessary, assign someone to check on them on a weekly basis. Second, there may need to be a ministry developed strictly for the senior members of the congregation. There are also organization, medical facilities and care facilities designed specifically for senior adults such as adult day cares and the elderly parent or grandparent is with others, doing activities and receiving meals when the other family members are at work.

Senior Ministries are a way that the entire church can support the older members of the church. With a Senior Ministry leader, there can be activities, coordinated meals and special events developed especially for the needs and desires of the seniors in the church.

Quality Facilities for their Adult Parents —The church can partner with assisted living, nursing home and transitional care facilities to have their representatives make actual presentations to the aging members and their families to answer questions, provide information and the resources that families need to make the correct decisions for their family member.

Although we have focused in this chapter on the aging and elderly, there are others who may come into our community who have been abandoned, alone, or single because of circumstances beyond their control. There may be single people that are alone because of job reassignment or relocation for one reason or another. They may have no family in the area and may or may not visit them on holidays because of financial restraints or even having the eligibility for time off. These people still must be acknowledged, checked in on and asked about possible holiday plans, any problems they may have settling in or getting acclimated to the area. They may have questions as to where is the best doctor, grocery store, hair dresser or dry cleaners? They may not have a financial need but just a socialization need. Are there some extrovert and outgoing young people in your church who can socialize and have great fun in a safe environment? Being able to include an alone person in your church's circle of youth and/or young adults can transform their lives and can turn a casual acquaintance into a church member for life. You never know. Jesus came to seek and to save those who were lost.(Luke 19:10)People at times feel lost in the world and all alone. Jesus is still the savior, but it is the church's responsibility at times, to go out of its way to seek out and ask those who are alone, "How are you doing and is there something that we can do to help?"

Finally, the church should not only be the family of God but, at times, the family for others. There may be times on a special occasion, an alone church member may spend a holiday with a family in the church or if they are not mobile, take a meal or two by the home to share the food and other amenities of the season. Jesus promised He would be with us always and never leave us nor forsake us, "….lo, I am with you always, even unto the end of the world. Amen." (Matthew 28:20)But as the church, we must be the hands and feet of Jesus to show love, care and kindness to all especially those who are aging, alone and/or at times, feel abandoned.

Reflection Page

Reflection Page

Chapter 7
The Family in Crisis

Historically, the Family has been in crisis since the beginning of the first family in the Garden of Eden with Adam and Eve. Eden was their paradise and designed to not only be their dwelling place but their protected place, worship and communion place with the Father and the place for their family. But because of disobedience and the fall of man, they no longer could dwell in that perfect paradise and unhindered relationship with God. When Adam and Eve were thrown out of Eden, the struggle, battle, warfare and crisis of the family really began. Sin entered the world, and the Bible says that God said, "I will put enmity between thee and the woman, and between thy seed and her seed; it shall bruise thy head, and thou shalt bruise his heel." (Genesis 3:15) The war began between the enemy and the woman, the helpmeet of the man and her seed, their children. The enemy has been looking to kill the seed of the woman but unable to do that because Jesus was born, the heir, the savior and redeemer of mankind. Jesus went to Calvary and conquered sin, hell and the grave but even after He rose and went back to Heaven, we are still here in warfare with the enemy. The enemy wants us to go with him to eternal death in Hell, but, thankfully, we have the Holy Spirit that dwells inside of us to lead, guide and empower us each and every day to help us live until we leave this earth. But in spite of the indwelling of the Holy Spirit, which we are eternally thankful for, it is still a war nevertheless.

Throughout the ages, long after Adam and Eve were buried, the family has endured, survived but is still in the fight to stay together and thrive. The family has been able to sustain itself through floods, catastrophes and the strife of ancient times, new land discoveries and expansion, 400 years of slavery and/or abuse inflicted on multiple ethnicities including the Jewish Holocaust, Hiroshima and nuclear bombings. There have been civil and world wars, famine, hatred, lynching, civil rights, disease, pestilence and natural disasters. We've seen the women's suffrage movement, the women's liberation movement, the women's equal pay movement that still remains a fight to this day for equal wages for equal work. Most people felt like women would never have babies or get married or even think of cooking ever again but that never stopped. We've seen men walk on the moon and women allowed to be astronauts and gone into space where they even went on missions with men into space. The family has still remained intact, there have been modifications on both sides as to who will care for the children and even how the children will be raised, but we still have families today. In 1967, the Lovings won against the State of Virginia to abolish interracial marriage being illegal, so there has been a high rate of interracial marriages and biracial children of all combinations. In

2008, we celebrated an African American United States President but who knew that even after that major accomplishment, the family would still have more crises to overcome.

For decades, our community, especially the African American community, has endured a high rate of incarceration as a result of very organized and strategic drug sales and distribution system, high alcohol use and divorce rate. Some parts of the world have more prevalent and wider spread drug trafficking than others. We are all affected by it.

Even though the world has gone through some horrific things, natural and supernatural, nothing has quite prepared us for the global pandemic. Now add to the pandemic, the unrest from the civil injustice of the criminal justice systems that has caused protests in the streets, It's nothing new. It's taken place in the past, but now it's televised. Now we see it live, up close as it happens. The evil is being recorded. Not even taping is necessary because people can go live and record what is happening as it happens. Coupled with advances in technology, you just need a phone. The phone records clearly, quickly and easily. When a person goes lives on social media, their followers and friends are notified so that they see what the person who is recording sees at the same time. Not to mention the people that they share to on social media that may not even be friends with the person doing the recording. In the end, the video is shared and can be seen by millions around the world in a matter of seconds. Multiple families and communities are affected by the crimes. The victim and assailant's families as well as anybody else who saw the video, live or on the replay can be affected. The older generations remember when that type of violence was only seen by a few and the tales were spread via the newspaper and word of mouth. The younger generations are angry, hurt and want immediate justice and take to the streets. The families are in crisis again because the parents want to protect their children and their children want to fight, march and see change. The unrest, the pandemic and uncertainty has put the family in higher crisis than what already existed.

What is the church's response to the current family in crisis and what are we to do?

First, we have to pray. Prayer is always in order and, again, the Bible teaches us to "Pray without ceasing." (1 Thessalonians 5:17) We have to pray for the victims. We pray for the criminals. The Bible tells us to pray for our enemies. So, we have to pray for those who despitefully use us and even the one who wanted us dead and/or wanted to destroy us.

Then second, the family is the foundation of everything related to mankind. After God created the light and all living things, God created man and woman and told them to be fruitful and multiply.(Genesis 1:26)So the family makes up the community, the community builds the cities, states, countries, continents, which is the entire world. As the family struggles in crisis, the entire world struggles and remains in crisis. Some families may be in financial crisis or emotional crisis. Some families are grieving, enduring the loss of loved ones and having to bury them in the midst of these multiple crises, which brings on financial, emotional and even spiritual crises. So, our job as a family is to stand together, comfort each other, care about each other and love each other. Whether we agree or not, vote for the same person or not, eat the same foods or not, love one another and realize our need for each other.

As the family is affected, the city is affected; as the countries and eventually the world. When the recent recorded crime against a young man in Minnesota happened, not only those in the United States marched against injustice but people around the world and in other countries also marched against the injustices in their part of the world. No matter how you look at it, we are all connected.

Next, we have to have some hard conversation with our children first about how their individual family will handle the crisis. We do not advocate destruction of property, destruction of businesses or any form of destructive retaliation during protests but it is because some people have not had conversations with their children on how to handle protests, injustice and anger in disagreeable situations. There should be conversations about what you should do, how you should handle yourself and what you should say or not say to authorities during these times. Through the conversations we can equip them. We must tell them what's right and what's wrong. Not only just in conversation but through actions behind the words you teach. Our families have to be taught prior to confrontation so they will know how to handle themselves in those situations. Today, you have to warn your children against the harmful, unsafe and dangerous world in which we live.

When families are in crisis, the church is in crisis. Therefore when the church is in crisis, we much rise to the occasion in the Word. We must rise in power, prayer, community, love and staying in communication and contact with each other. The technological age allows us to utilize all means necessary to stay connected, do ministry and get the word out. The Word says "go ye therefore into all the world and preach the gospel." (Matthew 28:19) Who knew in this time and era that going into "all the world" wasn't necessarily physical. Going into all of the world happens today via the Internet, technology and social media. We can easily and quickly go into all of the world without leaving our homes: just access the Internet. The Word can continue to move forward to comfort, heal, correct, discipline, help give information, enlighten, encourage and ultimately lead people to eternal salvation. So, the family in crisis is nothing new but the church family must rise to the occasion to help the local, national and international families in crisis to know Christ, receive His Power and Salvation to their souls before it is everlasting too late.

The family is still in crisis, but let us individually do what we can to solve the ills of this world, to mend the broken hearted, to comfort those that are bereaved, provide the information to those who need help by providing or pointing them to resources such as food, clothing, and shelter as well as being role models for the next generation.

As the family of God, we should continue to move forward, be strengthened by and walk in the Word so that we "may prosper and be in good health even as your soul prospers." (3 John 1:2 NKJV)

God created the family and it is His responsibility, Power and Might that are working through us to help encourage, cover in prayer and teach families everywhere through these and every other crisis.

Be Blessed and Encouraged.

Reflection Page

Reflection Page

About the Author

Pastor David L. Smith is a native of Houston, Texas, who surrendered his life to Christ and to His calling to serve His Kingdom, is a graduate of Mac Arthur High School with continued education at the College of Biblical Studies.

Currently as Pastor of New Bethlehem Missionary Baptist Church, and for more than 28 years, the Lord has granted him the ability to move individuals from membership to discipleship.

He has been married to his wife, Linda Smith for 35 years. They are the proud parents of three lovely daughters; Tamara, Crystal and Jessica and have three lovely granddaughters; Jayla, Tamia, Chandler and one grandson King David.

Pastor Smith worked and retired from the City of Houston as a Manager of Public Works & Engineering with over 31 years of service.

Pastor Smith's passion is to use his extraordinary gift of serving by assessing the immediate needs of his community.

Pastor David L. Smith has developed people for home ownership, financial stability, computer literacy, parenting, family enrichment, and health assessments.

In addition, Pastor Smith is a huge supporter and advocate for the Eastex-Jensen Community in which he serves as the president of the Houston Northeast CDC in which their primary goal is to promote Economic Development, Educate, Empower and Protect Our Community.

Board and Volunteer Experience

Position 6, Greater Northside Management District

Eastex Jensen Super Neighborhood #46 President

Past President & Board Member, Aldine Education Foundation

A great believer in community involvement, Pastor Smith is and has been very active in numerous associations including:

Member of PACA (Police and Clergy Alliance)

Community Advisory Board Member UT Physicians Multi-Specialty - Jensen

Crisis Chaplaincy of America

Precinct 1 CERT Team

Former Committee Member of Mayor Sylvester Turner's Public Safety Transitional Team

Former Board Member of Heritage Village Homeowners Association

Former Steering Committee Member of Aldine Independent School District

Former Volunteer and Mentor for the Buckner/Aldine Family Hope Center

Former Spring Independent School District Watch D.O.G.S (Dads of Great Students)

Former P.T.A Member of Aldine I.S.D.

About the Author

First Lady Linda H. Smith is a native of Smithfield, Virginia. She is the daughter of Robert & Virginia Hicks and the youngest of 3 siblings. She has been married to Pastor David L. Smith for 35 years and is the proud mother to three lovely daughters Tamara, Crystal and Jessica.

Linda adores her four grandchildren; three beautiful granddaughters Jayla, Tamia and Chandler along with one grandson King David.

She utilizes her gifts and talents in the areas of teaching, training and mentoring Christian women and young ladies. More specifically, she has taught and counseled women into confessing and repenting worldly sin while renewing the mind, and applying the Bible to their personal lives. Linda has a strong background in finance as well as organizing and offers assistance in managing time and finances by relating these subjects to and honoring the Word of God.

Linda is also a retiree of the Federal Reserve Bank Dallas, Houston Branch with 37 years of service in the financial industry.

Linda is the President of Building Lives Inc. a 501(c)3 non-profit organization which focuses on building people to be able to function at full capacity.

Board and Volunteer Experience

Position 2, City of Houston Tower Permit Commission Board

Member of Mayor Sylvester Turner's Prayer Team

Harris County Sheriff's Citizens Police Academy Class# 38

Crisis Chaplaincy of America

Harris County Precinct Alternate Presiding Judge

Eastex Jensen Super Neighborhood #46

Member of PACA (Police and Clergy Alliance)

Community Advisory Board Member

Precinct 1 CERT Team

Former P.T.A. Member of Aldine Independent School District

Former Tutor with Junior Achievement

www.ingramcontent.com/pod-product-compliance
Lightning Source LLC
Chambersburg PA
CBHW072202160426
43197CB00012B/2492